The Escape

A play by Geraldine McCaughrean

Illustrated by Laura Ellen Anderson

Narrator: Once, a wicked wizard stole a princess.

Princess: Help! Help me!

Narrator: A prince arrived to rescue her, riding his big chestnut horse.

Chestnut: That's me!

Prince: Jump on.

Narrator: Unfortunately the wizard saw them escaping, and he leaped onto **his** horse.

Midnight: That's me. My name's Midnight, but he just calls me "silly horse".

Wizard: I'm coming after you! Get going, silly horse!

Princess: Faster! Faster! He's catching up!

Prince: Gee up, Chestnut!

Chestnut: I'm doing my best.

Wizard: You'll never get away from me!

Midnight: No need to shout. I don't like riders who shout.

Princess: Stop at the next crossroads, Prince.

Prince: Why?

Princess: Just do it.

Chestnut: Thank you. I needed a rest.

Princess: May this little wishing spell
Make my prince into a well.

Narrator: The prince turned into a well.

Prince: Well, well!

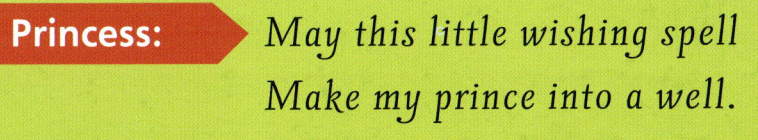

Narrator: Then the princess did some more magic.

Princess: *One more spell and then with luck, it will turn Chestnut into a bucket.*

Chestnut: Clank, clank.

Princess: *Cross my fingers, wish, and maybe, I'll become an old, old lady.*

Narrator: Soon the wizard came by.

Wizard: You there, old woman! Did you see a horse with two riders?

Princess: Oh yes, sir. They went that way.

Narrator: The wizard galloped off in the wrong direction.

Midnight: Stop kicking me! I don't like riders who kick!

Princess: Now undo magic, undo spell.
No more bucket, no more well.

Prince: Amazing! How did you do that?

Princess: I stole the wizard's wand, while I was a prisoner. Let's go!

Chestnut: Here we go again.

Narrator: The wizard was furious.

Wizard: Drat! I think I've been tricked. But I'll soon catch up.

Midnight: Ow! I don't like riders who shout **and** kick!

Princess: Faster! Faster! He's getting closer!

Prince: Gee up, Chestnut.

Chestnut: I'm doing my best.

Princess: Now STOP!
Abracadabra and one two three!
Chestnut – turn into a tree!

Prince: Hey – now my chestnut horse is a horse chestnut!

Princess: *Foul is fair and fair are fowl.*
Now I need a snowy owl.

Narrator: And the prince became an owl.

Prince: How did you do-woo-woo-woo that?

Princess: *Now I need a coat and hood*
And a big strong axe for chopping wood.

Prince: She's turned into a woodcutter.

Chestnut: Help! Don't chop me down!

Wizard: Whoa, beast.

Midnight: Go, stop. Stop, go. I don't like riders who can't make up their minds.

Wizard: You there, woodcutter! Did you see a horse with two riders?

Princess: They went that way, sir.

Narrator: So the wizard galloped off in the wrong direction again.

Princess: Now undo magic, undo please:
No more owls and no more trees.

Prince: Wow! How did you do that?

Princess: I learned the wizard's spells while I was a prisoner. Let's go.

Chestnut: Oh no, not again.

Narrator: The wizard was even more furious!

Wizard: Drat! I've been tricked again! Gallop, you lazy animal!

Midnight: Maybe I just I don't like wizards.

Princess: Faster! Faster! He's catching up.

Prince: Gee up, Chestnut.

Princess: Round this bend – and now the next one!

Chestnut: I'm getting dizzy!

Princess: STOP!

Prince: I'm feeling a bit green after all that.

Princess: That gives me an idea! Lie down.
Until the wizard gallops past,
I'll turn you into a field of grass,
Now, horse, before it's all too late,
Change into runny chocolate!
Next I'll use my magic power
And turn into a little flower.

Narrator: The wizard came galloping round the bend.

Wizard: Whoa, silly horse!

Midnight: He never says please, you know.

Wizard: Chocolate! A river of chocolate! I **love** chocolate!

Midnight: Grass is better. Mmmm.

Wizard: Mmmm. Chocolate!

Midnight: Grass ... and a little flower! How do flowers taste?

Princess: Oh dear!

Midnight: Shall I try it?

Princess: Oh dear, oh dear! If I change back now, the wizard will see me!

Wizard: Mmmmm. Yummy, yummy chocolate!

Princess: *Undo magic, undo charm,
Or else this flower will come to harm!*
Phew! That was close.

Prince: Wow! How did you make the wizard disappear?

Princess: While I was a prisoner, I learned how to make vanishing chocolate.

Prince: Look at me! I've been nibbled by that wizard's horse!

Princess: Well, never mind. You needed a haircut.

Prince: And look at Chestnut. He's shrunk.

Midnight: Pretty pony!

Chestnut: I am **not** a pony. I'm a horse.

Midnight: Pony.

Chestnut: Horse! I'm only small because your wizard drank some of me while I was chocolate.

Prince: Well, at least the princess is free now.

Princess: Yes – thanks for rescuing me, Prince. Goodbye!

Prince: Oh. Are you off home, then?

Princess: Of course. Only one little problem. I don't have a horse.

Chestnut: You think **you** have problems! I've been shrunk!

Midnight: And my owner has vanished!

Princess: Problems solved! The wizard's horse needs a new owner.

Midnight: Yes!

Princess: And the prince needs a larger horse.

Prince: I certainly do!

Princess: And I need a brave little pony to ride.

Chestnut: That's me, I suppose.

Prince: Shall we all go home now?